C000057951

THE

HAPPINESS

JOURNAL

vie

THIS JOURNAL BELONGS TO...

_____

INTRODUCTION

With the rapid pace of modern life, and the ever-increasing demands on us to be better, to have more and to work harder, we often forget about our mental well-being and how important it is to be happy. This journal encourages you to take a step back and be more mindful of the different aspects of your life, offering ways to boost your mood and achieve long-lasting happiness

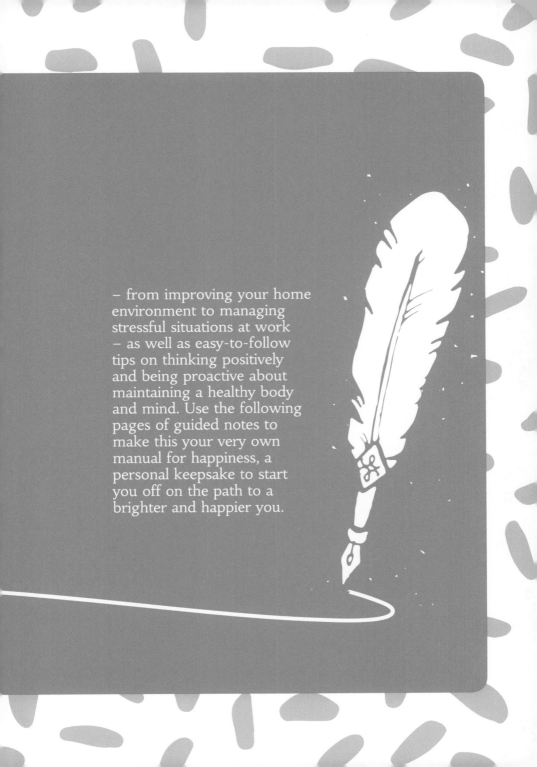

– from improving your home environment to managing stressful situations at work – as well as easy-to-follow tips on thinking positively and being proactive about maintaining a healthy body and mind. Use the following pages of guided notes to make this your very own manual for happiness, a personal keepsake to start you off on the path to a brighter and happier you.

Techniques for Being Happy

By picking up this journal
you've made a positive start in
your bid for lasting happiness.
By adjusting your lifestyle
and mindset in line with our
tips and simple techniques,
you'll start to be able to
allay anxieties and negative
thoughts by relaxing your
body and mind. In adding
your own thoughts, ideas and
comments within the spaces
provided, you'll find you start
to bring more harmony and
happiness into your life.

Happiness,
not in another
place but this
place, not for
another hour
but this hour.

Walt Whitman

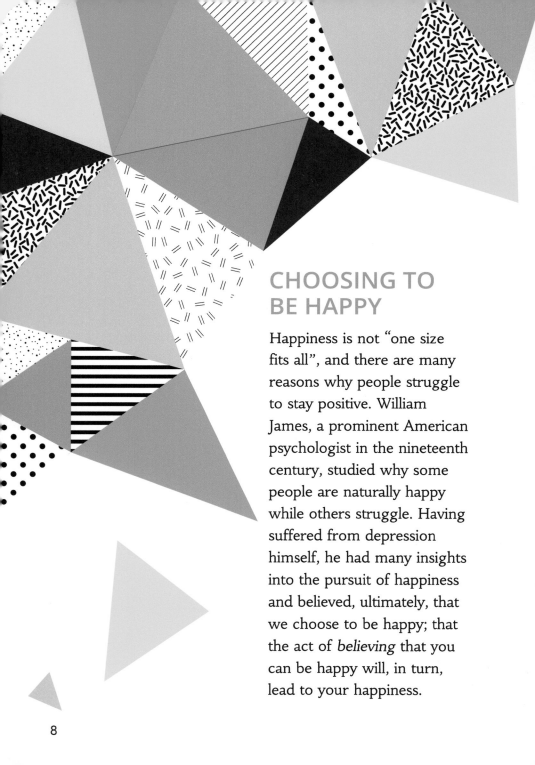

CHOOSING TO BE HAPPY

Happiness is not "one size fits all", and there are many reasons why people struggle to stay positive. William James, a prominent American psychologist in the nineteenth century, studied why some people are naturally happy while others struggle. Having suffered from depression himself, he had many insights into the pursuit of happiness and believed, ultimately, that we choose to be happy; that the act of *believing* that you can be happy will, in turn, lead to your happiness.

Think about a time when you were happy
and use the space provided to describe it:

What made it a happy experience? Choose some
words to describe how you felt, for example
"warm", "safe" and "loved" might come to mind.

_____   _____   _____

_____   _____   _____

_____   _____   _____

*Now immerse yourself in those happy
thoughts and believe that you can attain
that level of happiness again.*

HAPPINESS

IS BY CHOICE, NOT BY CHANCE.

Find your
own path to

happiness

and follow it.

Talk it out

Talking to a good friend (or friends) about your problems helps you to put your own worries in perspective, and, conversely, congratulating each other on the good things happening in your lives is a wonderful way to boost your happiness levels. When you're stuck in a negative spiral, talk to people who can put things into perspective and offer solutions, and if they can make you laugh at the same time, even better.

Write a list of things that are on your mind, and then write the name of someone you can share your worry with alongside it.

A

MULTITUDE

 OF

SMALL DELIGHTS

CONSTITUTE

 HAPPINESS.

Charles Baudelaire

Reasons to be cheerful, 1, 2, 3

Write down all the things in your life that put a smile on your face, such as spending time with family and friends, hobbies, pets or goals that you've reached. You'll quickly surprise yourself by how many things you can think of. Refer back to this page every day as a reminder of how good life is.

Research published in the Journal of Clinical Psychology found that those who adopted this habit of writing down positive aspects of their life became significantly happier.

One positive thought in the morning can change your whole day.

Start your day with good intentions

When you wake up, give yourself a goal or intention for the day before getting up.

It could be something as simple as "Stay calm at work" or "Be more productive" or "Enjoy working with my colleagues", but don't make it an actual "thing" to do, as this could cause anxiety.

_____

_____

_____

_____

_____

_____

_____

_____

_____

_____

_____

_____

_____

_____

Make a mood board

Mood boards aren't just for those who make art and interiors. A mood board can help you to stay focused on attaining your goals, and keep your mood buoyant. Start by gathering together beautiful images of places you want

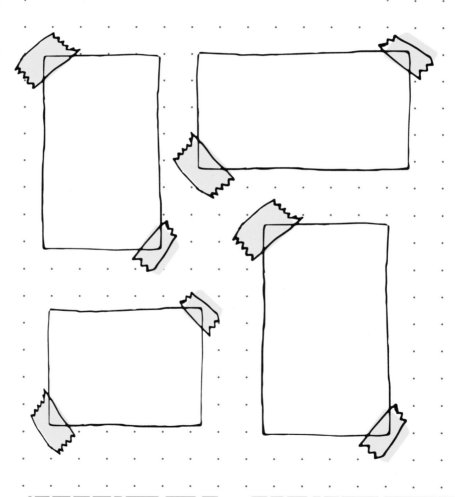

to visit, zingy colours and fabric swatches, and inspiring quotes and snippets of poetry that make you smile every time you read them. Use these pages to display your ideas.

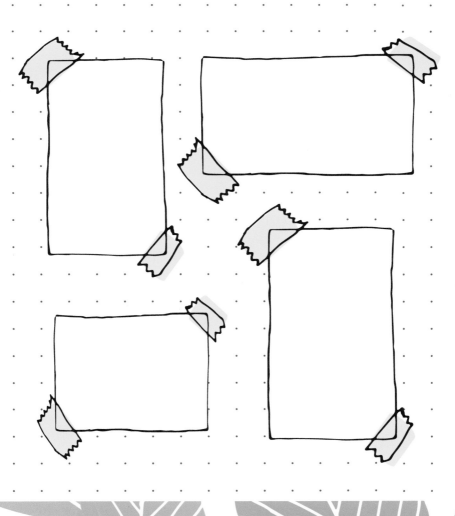

Smile!

Smiling releases endorphins, the body's natural feel-good chemicals. Even if you don't feel like it, turning up the corners of your mouth into a smile will give you a boost. Recent studies have shown that a person's mood begins to align with the emotion that their face is communicating, so show those pearly whites! It's also worth remembering the old adage that it takes fewer muscles to smile than frown.

Use this space to write down some jokes that really make you laugh, or memories that bring a smile to your face.

....

....

....

....

....

....

....

....

....

....

....

....

....

....

Very little is needed to make a happy life; it is all within yourself, in your way of thinking.

Marcus Aurelius

Keep challenging yourself

It may take years of patience and graft to master a skill, such as drawing well or learning a foreign language, but studies show that you have a greater chance of being happier day-to-day in the long term if you actively pursue a pastime or hobby. That feeling of losing yourself in study or a creative pursuit is referred to as "flow", and this state, according to some psychologists, is where true happiness lies.

Use this step-by-step guide on drawing a face to get your creative juices flowing, and use the following pages to build on your artistic ability. One day you can look back and see how far your skills have come!

1. Using a pencil, draw the shape of the head.

2. Halfway from the top, lightly draw a horizontal line (this is where the eyes will go).

3. Lightly draw a vertical line down the middle (this will help to keep the features in the right place).

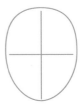

4. Halfway between the eyeline and the chin, draw a short line (this will become the nose).

5. Slightly above the halfway point between the nose and chin, draw a longer line (this will become the mouth).

6. Using an art pencil or pen for the next steps, draw two curves on the eyeline, and then study the eyes you are drawing and adjust the shape accordingly below the line.

7. Draw on a nose and a mouth, using your guidelines. Then add hair; remember: it needs to sit above and below the skull outline.

8. Erase all your pencil guidelines and there you have it!

Have a doodle!

Have a doodle!

Choose a job you love,
and you will never have to
work a day in your life.

Confucius

No matter
what has gone
before, you can
always take a
fresh step into a
hopeful future.

Steer your life toward happiness

Do you know what you want from your life? Are you happy in your work? What about your personal life? If your current situation is making you unhappy then it's time to make some changes. What could you change that might make you feel

My aspirations

more positive? Set realistic goals that help you feel inspired
and excited about making changes – and choose the goals
that are right for you, not ones to please anyone else.

**Write down your aspirations and try to adopt a realistic
plan for achieving them. If you fancy a career change,
why not take the first step by seeing a careers advisor
or getting work experience in your chosen field?**

Plan of action

- _____
- _____
- _____
- _____
- _____
- _____
- _____
- _____

- _____
- _____
- _____
- _____
- _____
- _____
- _____
- _____

**Tell yourself that by this time next year you'll be well on
the way to making positive and lasting changes in your life.**

Do not spoil what you have by desiring what you have not; but remember that what you now have was once among the things only hoped for.

Epicurus

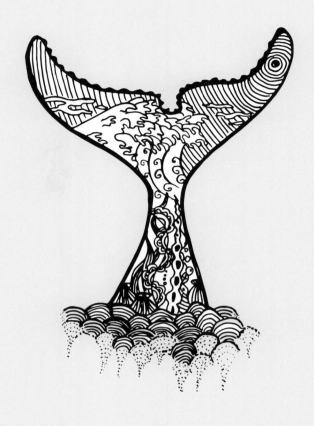

HAPPINESS IS ESSENTIALLY A
STATE OF GOING SOMEWHERE,
WHOLEHEARTEDLY, ONE-DIRECTIONALLY,
WITHOUT REGRET OR RESERVATION.

William Herbert Sheldon

Let go

We all have a habit of holding on to negative experiences, guilty feelings, regrets and bad friends. It's time to make a pact with yourself and let those negative things go, so you can move forward to a happier, brighter future. Sometimes it feels good to say, "No more!" or "I'm never doing that again!"

Start your campaign here:

Say "no" to...

_____

_____

_____

_____

_____

Goodbye to...

_____

_____

_____

_____

_____

No more...

Let go of...

Be you

Revel in what makes you different and follow your own path to happiness. Don't feel under pressure to do or be what others expect of you – because no one knows you better than you know yourself.

Fill in these inspiration bubbles with activity ideas that will make you happy – one step to realizing happiness is writing it down.

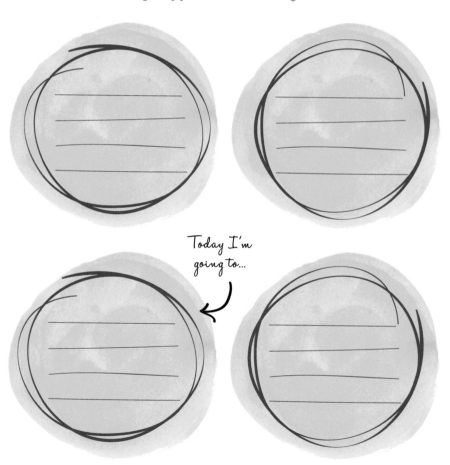

Today I'm going to...

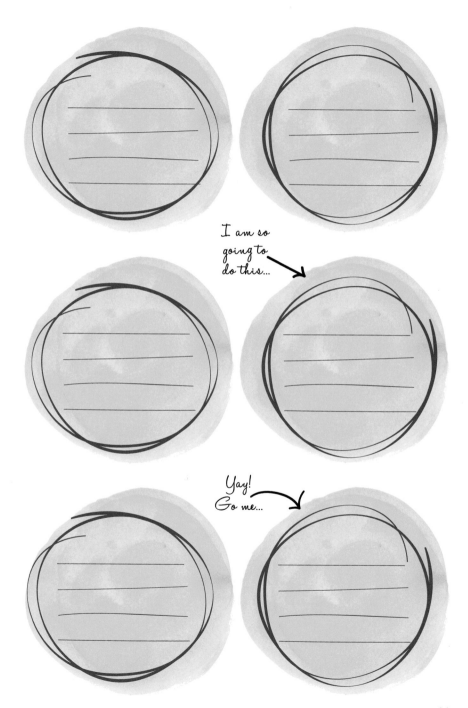

I am so
going to
do this...

Yay!
Go me...

Own your decisions

Sticking to a decision and having the courage of your convictions is a sure route to true happiness, because it makes you feel in control of your life and the master (or mistress) of your own destiny.

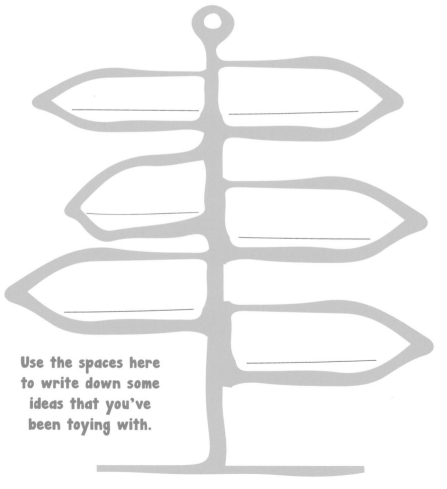

Use the spaces here to write down some ideas that you've been toying with.

Use this page to explore the ways in which
you could turn your ideas into actions.

Idea   **Action**

_____   _____

                     _____

                     _____

_____   _____

                     _____

                     _____

_____   _____

                     _____

                     _____

_____   _____

                     _____

                     _____

_____   _____

                     _____

                     _____

_____   _____

                     _____

                     _____

Don't compare yourself to others

Continually striving for perfection, which in itself is an impossible goal, will prevent you from being happy, and deny you the opportunity to feel good about everything you have achieved. One of the most common traits of perfectionism is comparing yourself with others, such as feeling inferior because someone has a better job, a bigger house or more money than you, which steers you away from looking at all the positive things happening in your life. Everybody is on their own journey; just try to be the best version of you.

Take the opportunity to recognize and list what you are good at, and areas in your life that could be improved. Writing these things down can help you to see where you are on your own journey — how far you're come, and where you want to go next.

Things I'm
good at

_____   _____
_____   _____
_____   _____
_____   _____
_____   _____
_____   _____
_____   _____
_____   _____
_____   _____

Areas I'd like
to improve

REPEAT THIS MANTRA:

I AM RESPONSIBLE FOR MY OWN HAPPINESS.

I AM RESPONSIBLE FOR MY OWN HAPPINESS. I AM RESPONSIBLE FOR MY OWN I AM HAPPINESS. RESPONSIBLE FOR MY OWN HAPPINESS. I AM RESPONSIBLE FOR MY OWN HAPPINESS.

Happiness tips

Whenever you're feeling low, refer back to these pages to remind yourself of the importance of self-care and making your own happiness.

Make time for yourself

It's very easy to forget your own needs when you lead a busy life full of responsibilities. Allocate time to yourself on a regular basis – even blocking out time on your calendar as "me time" – to just do the things that you enjoy or to sit and think or meditate and appreciate your own company.

The best things in life are free!

Research has shown that simple experiences like dipping your toes in the sea or having a cup of tea in the sunshine affords far greater pleasure than attaining material goods, so rather than hitting the shops for retail therapy when you need a happiness boost, head outside for some free mood-lifting entertainment!

Enjoy a treat every day

If you're feeling sad, tense or anxious, try doing something nice – however small – every day to give yourself a happiness boost. Whether it's making a sumptuous dessert to have with your dinner, going to bed early to read a book, enjoying a long soak in the bath or meeting a friend for coffee, having something to look forward to will help you remain positive throughout the day. Look through your diary and make sure you have treats booked in at regular intervals to keep you happy. The treats don't even need to cost any money – if it's sunny, head out to the park with a friend and take some tennis rackets and a ball; if it's cold, look for free events in your local area or visit a friend.

Sing for joy

Singing provides a wonderful happiness boost and it's a great stress reliever too – it's hard to sing and feel stressed at the same time! It's also good for your health as it releases "feel good" endorphins and the deep breathing required increases oxygen levels in the blood. Another positive aspect of singing is that it improves posture and tones your tummy. Singing in a choir or singing group is even more rewarding as it's a great way to make friends and have fun at the same time – see www.naturalvoice.net for choirs in your locale.

49

Be generous

According to research, money *can* buy happiness, but only if you spend it on someone other than yourself. It's win-win, because not only will you make someone else feel special, but by doing so, you'll make yourself happy too!

Don't let anyone make you feel bad

It's important to recognize the people in your life who feed your negative thinking, or belittle you. Don't feel obliged to spend time with them – life is too short to waste time on people who don't have your best interests at heart.

SMILE AND THE WORLD WILL SMILE BACK.

Visualize a happier you

When starting out on your journey to lasting happiness, it can be hard to see what the end result will be. It is easy to be put off by the "what if"s a situation might bring to mind, and this is where creative visualization can help. Find a comfortable chair to sit in and relax. Begin by closing your eyes and focusing on the natural rhythm of your breathing. Next, start to build up a picture in your head of how a happier, more content you would look and behave. Where are you? Who is beside you in this happy place? Notice every detail and enjoy how it feels. While you are working on becoming happier with your life, carry this mental image with you as inspiration.

Use the space on the opposite page to draw what you are visualizing so that you can easily refer back to it and reawaken the positive image.

An act to make
another happy
inspires the other to
make still another
happy, and so
happiness is aroused
and abounds.

Buddha

The gift of giving

Doing things for others is not only a great way to take your mind off problems — it also feels good. One recent study concluded that those who volunteer for selfless reasons live longer, and altruism is also linked to stronger and happier relationships. There are many ways that you can volunteer your free time, such as helping out at a local charity. Closer to home, consider visiting someone you know who doesn't have family nearby and would appreciate some company, or offer to do the supermarket shop for an elderly neighbour.

Jot down some ideas about
how you could start a
concerted giving campaign.

Always be a
first-rate version
of yourself,
instead of a
second-rate
version of
somebody else.

Judy Garland

The best way
to cheer yourself
is to try to
cheer somebody
else up.

Mark Twain

Book an experience or holiday with friends

Think about holidays or days out that you've spent with friends and the stories that you still talk about when you get together. Shared experiences are proven to offer greater, longer-lasting happiness, as the experiences can be reminisced about for years to come – the things that go wrong often provide the funniest memories! And it's not just the enjoyment of the experience and the ability to reminisce about them; it's also the planning and anticipation that makes us feel positive and happy. As if you needed any excuse to start researching that next trip!

Plan some dream outings,
excursions or holidays here.

A JOY AIRED IS A JOY SHARED.

Friends

are the artists

who paint

happy lips

on your face.

Richelle E. Goodrich

ORGANIZE A MOVIE NIGHT

Host a movie night for a group of friends. Pick your favourite comedy to ensure plenty of laughs and don't forget the popcorn!

Make a list of the funniest movies you would like to share:

_____

_____

_____

_____

_____

_____

_____

_____

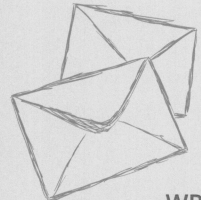

WRITE A LETTER

Most of us have relatives or friends who live at the other end of the country, or have even emigrated. Give yourself (and them) a boost by sitting down to write a letter by hand, letting them know what you've been up to and asking them plenty of questions. Use this as an opportunity to catch up in a way you wouldn't be able to over the phone or via Facebook, by being honest and open, and perhaps sending a little memento such as a photograph along with your note. You will most likely get a handwritten reply, too, which will add to the sense of joy and satisfaction.

12.6.07

26,-

Who will be the lucky recipients? Make a list of all the people you'd like to write to here:

_____

_____

_____

_____

_____

_____

_____

_____

_____

Give compliments

Giving or receiving a heartfelt compliment boosts
self-esteem and happiness levels – so make the effort
to make someone's day. Tell them how great they look
or how much you like and admire something about
them (e.g. a personality trait). If a work colleague has
submitted an impressive report thank them sincerely
– chances are you'll receive a compliment back.

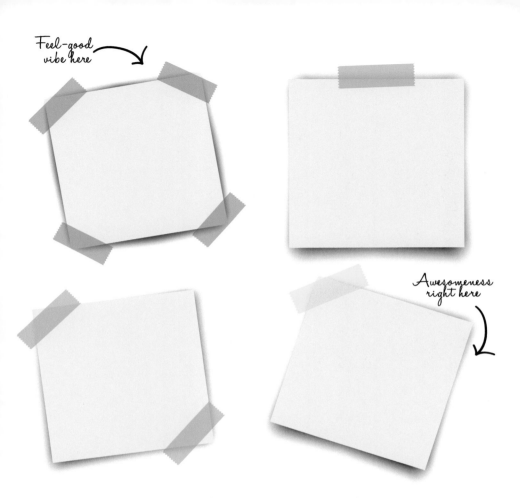

Feel-good vibe here

Awesomeness right here

Be sure to thank someone when they have given you a compliment and take a moment to truly enjoy what has been said. In the same way, save complimentary emails, cards and messages, and file away your best performance reviews at work. Re-read these words whenever you need a boost.

Write down compliments you've received on the sticky notes above.

REMEMBER BIRTHDAYS

Sending a thoughtful card, email or gift on someone's birthday means you'll be in touch with the people that matter most at least once a year – a good start for building and maintaining important relationships.

Name: _____

Date: _____

Name: _____

Date: _____

Name: _____

Date: _____

Name: _____

Date: _____

Name: _____

Date: _____

Name: _____

Date: _____

Name: _____

Date: _____

Name: _____

Date: _____

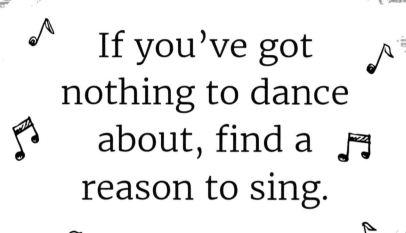

If you've got nothing to dance about, find a reason to sing.

Melody Carstairs

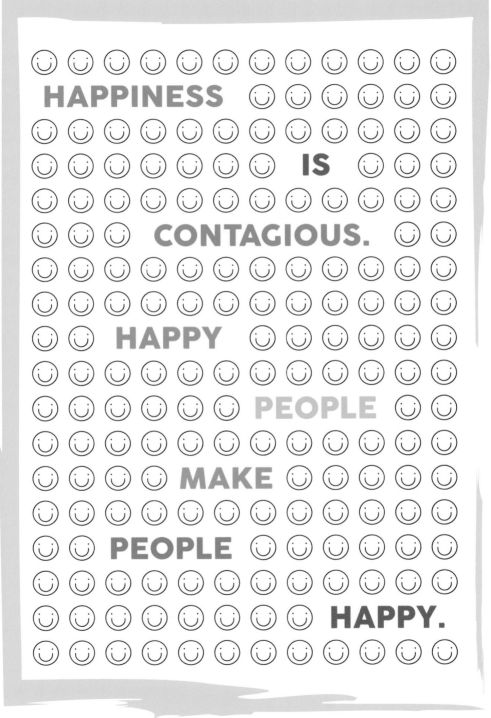

HAPPINESS IS CONTAGIOUS. HAPPY PEOPLE MAKE PEOPLE HAPPY.

Happiness tips

Making other people happy can bring a significant amount of joy to our own lives. Refer back to this page when you feel that you or those around you need their spirits buoyed.

Make a phone call

Call up one person a day for a catch-up or a gossip – studies show that even if we're having an off day, speaking to a loved one will make us feel happier.

Give someone a hug

A good hug is one of the quickest ways to boost happiness levels as it encourages the flow of oxytocin, which soothes your nervous system, lowering blood pressure and stress levels.

Walk a dog for a friend or family member

Offering to walk someone's dog frees up time for them to do more for themselves, while giving you the opportunity to get out into nature with an animal companion. Dog-walking is a positive experience for both you and the pet; not only does it offer the chance for some green exercise for both you and the dog, but it is well known that spending time with animals provides a mood boost.

Nothing can make our life, or the lives of other people, more beautiful than perpetual kindness.

Leo Tolstoy

HAPPINESS IN THE HOME

Home should be the one place where you feel happiest and most relaxed. If you find that it has become a source of stress, the following tips will help you to turn your home back into a place of joy, comfort and calm.

Having a tidy, home with clear surfaces and a place for everything is important for general happiness and well-being. A clutter-free environment is calming, and the act of tidying can be satisfying too. Try conducting a wardrobe audit to get you started on a path to a less cluttered life.

Answer the following questions before you begin
your audit, to help you focus your mind on what is
important to you and what you hope to achieve:

**1. Why do you want to
do a wardrobe audit?**

_____

_____

**2. What three words
do you want to
describe your style?**

_____

_____

_____

**3. What three words actually
describe your style?**

_____ _____ _____

**5. How many items do
you actually have?**

**4. How many items do
you think you have in
your wardrobe?**

**7. What does your
wardrobe need?**

_____

**6. What do you
own enough of?**

_____

_____

8. What can you get rid of?

_____

**9. What do you hope to
achieve from this process?**

_____

**10. How will you
feel afterwards?**

_____

When you love what you have, you have everything you need.

Get moneywise

If you leave your bank statements and bills unopened because of the fear of what lies within, then it's time to get organized and wise up to your finances for your own sanity and long-term happiness. Begin by creating a simple spreadsheet of your monthly income and expenditure. If you're finding that you run out of money mid-month, there might be some very simple, pain-free cutbacks that you can make.

Use this simple spreadsheet to start logging your spending this month, so that you can begin to get a rough picture of where your money goes.

DATE	SHOP	ITEM(S)	COST

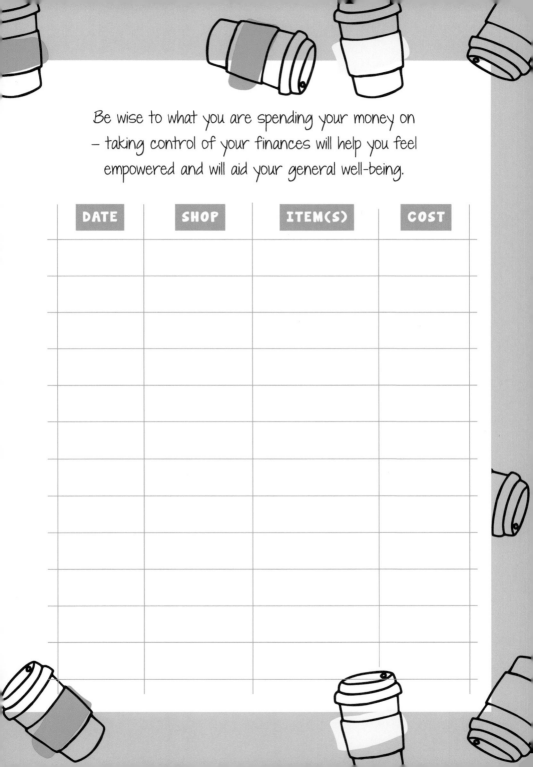

Be wise to what you are spending your money on
– taking control of your finances will help you feel
empowered and will aid your general well-being.

DATE	SHOP	ITEM(S)	COST

The true secret of happiness lies in taking a genuine interest in all the details of daily life.

William Morris

You are
what you do,
not what
you have.

Laughter is the best medicine

Laughter is good for you; not only does it release endorphins which make you feel happy, but there are proven health benefits too. A good belly laugh is akin to a mild workout session, because it gets the blood flowing and the muscles working. It also reduces stress hormones and blood pressure, gives your immune system a boost, improves memory and has a positive effect on sleep patterns.

Use this page to note down your favourite funny memories and moments. Refer back to them when you are feeling low for an instant mood boost.

Funniest memories with friends:

_____

_____

Favourite funny TV show:

_____

_____

Favourite comedy films:

_____

_____

Funniest jokes you've ever heard:

_____

_____

Funniest YouTube videos:

_____

_____

One of the best ways to make yourself happy in the present is to reminisce on happy times from your past.

DON'T TAKE YOURSELF TOO SERIOUSLY

– LEARN TO LAUGH AT YOURSELF.

Learn to unplug

It's the easiest thing to come home after a day at work and sit in front of the TV, regardless of whether there is something you actually want to watch or not, or go online and lose yourself in social media. Before you know it, hours

_____   _____

_____   _____

_____   _____

_____   _____

_____   _____

_____   _____

_____   _____

_____   _____

_____   _____

_____   _____

Have some healthy snacks on your desk

When you are in need of an extra shot of energy at work, it can be tempting to reach for unhealthy sugary snacks, but after the initial sugar rush is over you can start to feel low and sluggish. Try fresh fruit, nuts, popcorn or a small amount of dark chocolate instead – these will help maintain energy levels and a healthy mind and body.

Stretch

Sitting down all day and working at a computer can lead to health complaints, such as eye strain, headaches, weight gain and low mood. Try to stretch every so often, or if you're on a short break, run up and down stairs or get outside and take a short walk.

Learn to say "no"

Be realistic about your workload. If you are one of those people who always say "yes" to taking on tasks for fear of looking bad by refusing simply be realistic and have the courage to say when enough is enough.

Associate with people who
are likely to improve you.

Seneca

Recipes

have passed and the evening is over. Shake up your routine. Rather than reaching for the remote, tablet or smartphone, make time for hobbies you love, invite friends round or go on a date night with your partner — you'll soon feel excited about coming home with so many things to look forward to.

Make a list of activities you could do instead of being obsessed by your phone.

Nothing
great was ever
achieved without
enthusiasm.

Ralph Waldo Emerson

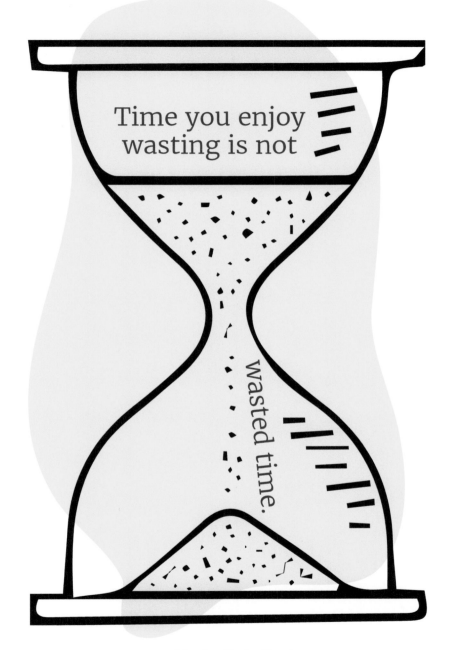

Time you enjoy wasting is not wasted time.

Marthe Troly-Curtin

Happiness tips

Getting the right amount of sleep can do wonders for your mood. Refer back to these pages if you ever find yourself struggling to get some good quality rest.

Sleep well, feel well

It's no surprise that being tired is not conducive to happiness. Lack of sleep weakens the immune system, slows reaction times and makes us more prone to depression, anxiety and low mood. Seven hours' sleep a night is generally regarded as the minimum amount required in order to remain healthy. The following tips will encourage a better night's sleep so that you feel energized and positive at the start of each new day.

Listen to classical music before bed

Studies have shown that listening to classical music lowers body temperature and heart rate and calms your breathing, which is ideal for inducing a restful night's sleep.

Make your bedroom a happy zone

Your bedroom should be a sanctuary – a place for sleep and sex only. Keep it devoid of clutter, open the windows for a period each day to allow fresh air to flow through, and regularly change the bedding, to keep it crisp, fresh and inviting. Keep your phone out when you retire to sleep.

Practise meditation

Brain scans have shown that Buddhist monks, who practise regular meditation, have happiness levels that are off the charts. Studies have shown that those who meditate for 10 minutes a day sleep better and are happier and more resilient when it comes to handling stress.

Clear your mind before sleep

One of the most common factors of sleep deprivation is worry. It's important to clear your mind of negative thoughts before you go to bed. There are a number of ways to do this, such as writing down what's on your mind or compiling a to-do list for the next day.

A comfortable home is a great
source of happiness. It ranks
immediately after health
and a good conscience.

Sydney Smith

Only surround yourself with things that bring joy to your heart.

Happiness tips

On the whole, most of us spend more of our waking hours at work than we do at home. With this in mind, it's especially important to be happy at work so refer back to these pages when you feel in need of a boost.

Make friends at work

Having a workmate to chat to by the water cooler or to go out to lunch with can make your working day much happier, and more fun! Make plans to go out for lunch or to the cinema every so often so that you can get to know your colleagues.

Say "thank you"

Take the time to thank people when they have done a job well – it will brighten someone's day and spread a happy vibe around the office.

Don't multitask

According to research, multitasking wastes more time than it saves, and it is destructive to a person's creativity and concentration levels. When you have a multitude of jobs, create a list of priorities and focus on one job at a time.

TAKE TIME TO DO WHAT MAKES YOUR SOUL HAPPY.

Focus on
the positives

Every job has its ups and downs, but it's important to remember every now and then just how fortunate you are to be employed and to have the money and freedom to enjoy the time that you're not at work.

Use this page to note down all the things that you love about your job, and refer back to this page if ever you feel stuck in a rut, or weighed down by the negatives.

It might also help to think about where your current job might take you in the future, to remember that even if you're not enjoying every aspect of your career now, it is merely a stepping stone on the way to bigger and better things for you.

Use this page to write down some of your ambitions and career goals. Refer back to this page when you need some motivation to give it your all at work.

There is no duty we so
much underrate as the
duty of being happy.

Robert Louis Stevenson

KEEP CALM AND STAY POSITIVE.

Happiness tips

Eating is one of the great pleasures of life, but choosing the food that's going to maximize our energy and our happiness levels isn't always easy. Refer back to these tips when you feel you're not getting the most out of your food, to remind yourself what a powerful tool food can be towards positivity.

Go nuts

Eating two Brazil nuts a day will give you your daily dose of selenium, which is vital for healthy thyroid function. This will improve your mood and significantly decrease anxiety levels.

Drink water

Six to eight glasses of water is important for mental health, well-being and happiness. This is because water carries nutrients to our body's cells and flushes the toxins out. Dehydration leads to confusion and irritability.

Cut out caffeine

If you're prone to anxiety and low mood, it's advisable to cut caffeine from your diet. Some scientists believe that caffeine is the single most important cause of anxiety and that more than nine cups of coffee a day can cause extreme stress and panic attacks.

Eating for joy

Foods rich in minerals, vitamins and fatty acids are not only good for you but they have also been shown to lessen symptoms of depression and anxiety. Studies in how the food we consume affects mood have concluded that there are ten key nutrients that combat low mood and make us feel good.

Keep your GI low

A low-GI diet can have many health benefits – more steady energy levels, less bloating, no sugar cravings – all of which can help you to stay feeling positive. GI stands for glycaemic index: the ranking of carbohydrate-containing foods based on their overall effect on blood glucose levels. Eating low-GI foods – such as beans, rye bread and most fruit and veg – helps ensure your body is fuelled throughout the day and night, avoiding the spikes and dips in your blood sugar that can have a negative effect on your emotions.

Get happy with wholegrains

While it can be tempting to reach for a slice of cake or a biscuit when negativity strikes, it's important to remember that the combination of sugar and refined flour in these foods can be detrimental to health and cause a wide variety of problems. These issues range from skin conditions to serious illnesses, such as diabetes, all of which can cause your mood to dip.

Get the right balance of EFAs (essential fatty acids)

Getting the right amount of omega-3 in your diet is important for maintaining a healthy mind and a positive outlook. Simple steps for doing this include eating two portions of oily fish a week, or by sprinkling a tablespoon of seeds (pumpkin and sunflower) onto cereal or salad every day.

FOOD MAGNESIUM FOLATE IRON B6 CALCIUM VITAMINS B12 POSITIVITY FEEL GOOD ZINC HAPPINESS OMEGA-3 FRUIT CHROMIUM FATTY ACIDS VITAMIN D

Eat for Health and long-lasting happiness.

MAX YOUR MINERALS

Minerals are essential for a healthy nervous system, so to ensure general physical and mental well-being, it's important to include them in your diet.

CALCIUM maintains healthy blood vessels and strong bones – low levels of calcium are linked to low mood, particularly in women. Calcium is found in dairy products as well as kale and collard greens.

CHROMIUM is vital for regulating insulin in the body and it also helps the brain to regulate moods, the lack of it leading to an increased risk of high blood pressure and depression. Chromium can be found in broccoli, turkey, potatoes and wholegrain products.

MAGNESIUM plays an important role in the body's production of serotonin, without which there is the risk of a predisposition to stress and irritability. Magnesium is present in nuts, dark, leafy vegetables, fish and wholegrain products.

ZINC is a great mood balancer and is known to reduce symptoms of depression. It can be found in seafood, eggs, beans, mushrooms, nuts, seeds and kiwi fruit.

IRON transports oxygen around the body and strengthens muscle. Depleted levels lead to fatigue, low mood and depression. Iron deficiency is more common in women, and vegetarians might want to consider taking a supplement; find iron in dark-green leafy vegetables, meat, fish, beans, pulses, nuts and wholegrain products.

Recipes

Use the following pages to write down your
favourite mood-boosting recipes, so that you
always have some happy, tasty food ideas
on hand when you're feeling down.

Recipes

Recipes

_____

_____

_____

_____

_____

_____

_____

_____

_____

_____

_____

_____

_____

_____

_____

_____

_____

_____

you can be happy
- just believe it.

Happiness comes from within.

MOODS AND BOOZE

After a long day at the office many people reach for a glass of wine to help them unwind and de-stress. Alcohol is widely known to have a calming effect, as it releases endorphins (the body's natural feel-good drug), but this is negated by the depressant qualities of alcohol and the feeling of anxiety that can be left behind once the effects wear off. Try to cut down on alcohol in general, but if you do fancy a tipple, opt for a glass of Chianti, Merlot or Cabernet Sauvignon, as the grape skins used in these wines are rich in the sleep hormone melatonin.

Take an average week and fill in the chart below to
help you plot out your approximate alcohol intake.

When you start writing it down and working out the units it can
be a bit of a shock. However, taking stock of what you're really
drinking will help you realize where you could cut down a little,
and feel all the positive benefits of a less boozy-lifestyle.

Day of the week	Drink (Y/N)	Type of drink(s)	Amount	Units (approx.)
Monday				
Tuesday				
Wednesday				
Thursday				
Friday				
Saturday				
Sunday				

KNOW YOUR UNITS

Men and women are advised not to drink more
than 14 units a week on a regular basis.

Shot of spirits: ~1 unit

Alcopop: ~1.5 units

Small glass of wine: ~1.5 units

Bottle of lager/cider/beer: ~1.7 units

Can of lager/cider/beer: ~2 units

Medium glass of wine: ~2.1 units

Large glass of wine: ~3 units

NOW IS THE TIME TO BE HAPPY!

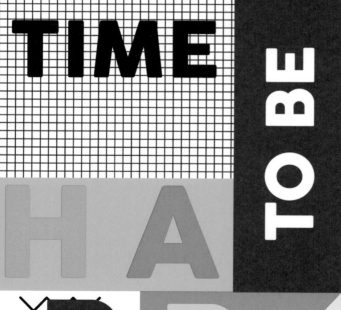

122

Optimism is the faith that leads to achievement; nothing can be done without hope.

Helen Keller

Happiness tips

Have you ever noticed how good you feel after a swim, a brisk walk or a jog? It's the release of the "happy" chemicals, endorphins and dopamine, and the reduction in the stress hormones cortisol and adrenalin, that makes you feel so good. According to research, just 20 minutes of exercise can boost your mood for up to 12 hours. Refer back to these pages if you ever feel in need of some mood-boosting exercise ideas.

A breath of fresh air

Studies show that people have a happier outlook if they spend time in nature. Breathing in fresh air and feeling the sun on your face is a wonderful quick fix of vitamin D. Inhaling deep breaths clears your lungs and increases the amount of oxygen being transported around your body, which, in turn, leads to a clearer mind and greater energy.

Practise yoga

The ancient practice of yoga is not just about bending your body, but also about balancing your mood. Yoga is practised at your own pace, allowing you to take time to really understand what your body can do. The calming effect it has on the mind and the physical effects of toning and strengthening the body can help increase your contentment levels.

Dance your way to happiness

Dancing is great fun and it's also a good workout. You could try a class: jive, jazz, ballroom and Latin classes are all great ways to get fit and meet new people, and fitness fusion classes such as Zumba are becoming ever more popular. Choose a style that suits you and, above all, enjoy it.

Go wild

Try wild swimming in a lake or the sea to experience nature while exercising. The health benefits of immersing yourself in cold water include the soothing of aches and pains and relief from depression and anxiety, as well as providing a boost to your immune system and vitality. The endorphin high from wild swimming makes you feel positive and happy, and ready to take on life's challenges.

Happiness is a journey, not a destination.

Proverb

No Matter
How Long
The Winter,
Spring
Is Sure
To Follow.

EXERCISE WITH FRIENDS

If you're struggling to get motivated to do some exercise, try pairing up with a friend to go jogging or have a round of tennis. Alternatively, join a class or team and rediscover sports that you enjoyed at school, such as netball, football or rugby, or try something new and exciting, like trampolining or rock climbing. Exercising with friends or in a group means that you can motivate each other and have fun at the same time.

Make a wish-list of the sports that you would like to practise and write down the details of local clubs you could contact to start joining in. No excuses now!

He who enjoys doing
and enjoys what he
has done is happy.

Johann Wolfgang von Goethe

LET YOUR

HAPPINESS

RADIATE
LIKE THE
SUN.

LISTEN TO MUSIC
WHILE YOU EXERCISE

Studies have shown that listening to
high-energy music while exercising
boosts your mood and makes the
workout seem easier. Similarly, watching
a favourite show while running on
a treadmill makes the activity much
more pleasant than staring at yourself
getting sweaty in the mirror!

Write down a playlist of the most motivating tunes you'd like to get moving to. Two classics to get you started: "Eye of the Tiger" by Survivor and "Fighter" by Christina Aguilera.

Song	Artist

Think BIG,

dream

BIGGER.

Now and then it's good to pause in our pursuit of happiness and just be happy.

Guillaume Apollinaire

Try positivity mantras

A mantra is a positive phrase that you repeat to yourself.
Mantras can be thought quietly in your head, or said out loud.
Many people believe that actually saying your mantra makes
it more effective, as vocalizing something gives it more
substance. You can also write down your chosen mantra

Mantras for calm

....
....
....
....

Mantras for motivation

....
....
....
....
....

Mantras for confidence

....
....
....

Mantras for gratitude

....
....
....

and put it somewhere you are likely to see it, such as the kitchen or bathroom. Choose your mantra based on what is important to you, not what you feel others will accept; it could be anything, from "I will pass my exam" to "I am a good, honest person". Regularly repeating your chosen mantra will help you reaffirm your faith in yourself and your abilities.

In these bubbles, write down some mantras that you could say to yourself.

Mantras for happiness

....

....

....

....

....

....

Mantras for acceptance

....

....

....

Mantras for self-belief

....

....

....

....

....

The present moment is filled
with joy and happiness. If you
are attentive, you will see it.

Thích Nhất Hạnh

Look in the mirror
and pay yourself
a compliment :

you are
wonderful!

AND FINALLY... DOCTOR'S ORDERS

If your low mood is having a negative effect on your day-to-day life, it is worth booking an appointment with your doctor to talk about it. Although complementary therapies can be effective, some situations need medical help. It may be that your doctor recommends a talking therapy such as CBT (cognitive behavioural therapy) or medication to help you. Remember the doctor is there to help, not to judge; tell them everything, and that way they will be able to give you the best possible advice.